BABY BLUES® SCRAPBOOK NUMBER 7

I SAW ELVIS IN MY ULTRASOUND

BABY BLUES® SCRAPBOOK NUMBER 7

I SAW ELVIS IN MY ULTRASOUND

By Rick Kirkman and Jerry Scott

Andrews and McMeel
A Universal Press Syndicate Company
Kansas City

ISBN: 0-8362-2130-3

Library of Congress Catalog Card Number: 96-83999

To Abbey. — JS
For Sir Tay & Mad Dog. — RK

Other Baby Blues Scrapbooks from Andrews and McMeel

Guess Who Didn't Take a Nap?
I Thought Labor Ended When the Baby Was Born
We Are Experiencing Parental Difficulties . . . Please Stand By
Night of the Living Dad

BABY BLUES

BY RICK KIRKMAN / JERRY SCOTT

12

BABY BLUES®

by RICK KIRKMAN / JERRY SCOTT

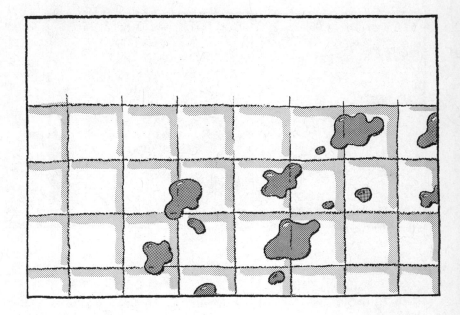

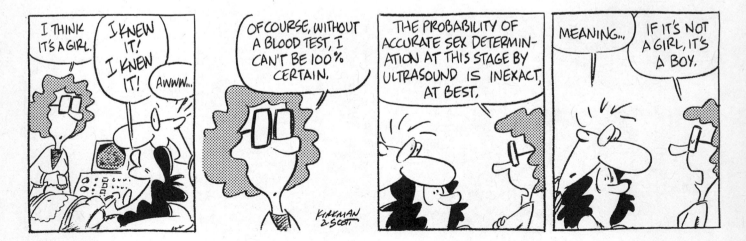

27

28

BABY BLUES®

BY RICK KIRKMAN / JERRY SCOTT

37

43

HEE HEE HA HA HA GIGGLE

WONK!

OWWWW!

WHAT HAPPENED??

ZOE ACCIDENTLY SMASHED MY NOSE WITH THE BACK OF HER HEAD!

OH, DEAR!

IS SHE HURT?

Z Z

OOOH! OWW! OWWW!

SORRY.

NO PROBLEM.

I DON'T KNOW WHO THESE LEG CRAMPS ARE HARDER ON...YOU OR ME.

I VOTE "ME".

BRRR! IT LOOKS CHILLY OUT THERE!

THIS WOULD BE A GOOD DAY TO PUT ON A WARM FUZZY SWEATSUIT AND SPEND THE DAY SIPPING COCOA AND PLAYING GAMES ON THE LIVING ROOM FLOOR

DOESN'T THAT SOUND NICE?

YES.

I WASN'T TALKING TO YOU.

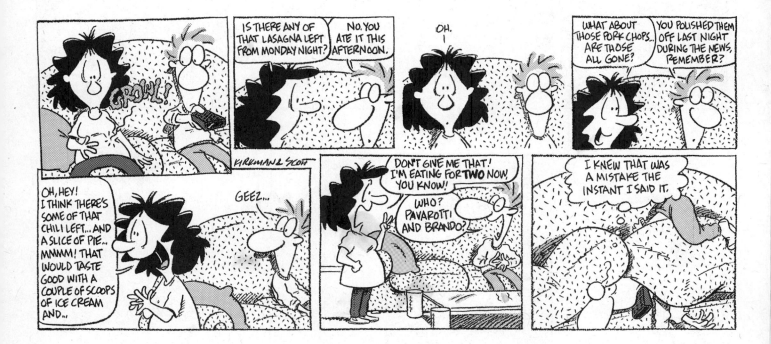

BABY BLUES®

RICK KIRKMAN / JERRY SCOTT BY

BABY BLUES®

Rick Kirkman BY Jerry Scott

THE FOUR SEASONS:

WINTER

OUR DAUGHTER HAS COLIC.

SPRING

OUR SON JUST STARTED SOLID FOOD.

SUMMER

OUR DAUGHTER IS TEETHING.

FLU

:SNIFF!: OUR SON HAS STARTED :HACK!: PRESCHOOL.

KIRKMAN & SCOTT

Row 1:

UH...

BABY HICCUPS.

THANK GOODNESS... FOR A MINUTE, I THOUGHT I NEEDED A NEW PRESCRIPTION.

KIRKMAN & SCOTT

Row 2:

 I'M SO GLAD I'M DOING ALL OF MY CHRISTMAS SHOPPING BY CATALOG.

 NO CROWDED MALLS... NO CRABBY SALES CLERKS... NO DANGEROUS PARKING LOTS.

 THIS YEAR, IT'S JUST GOING TO BE ME, THE TELEPHONE...

 ... AND THE EVER-PRESENT THREAT OF AN AVALANCHE.

KIRKMAN & SCOTT

Row 3:

TODAY ON "MOTHERS AND TODDLERS," WE'RE GOING TO SHOW SOME HOLIDAY CRAFT PROJECTS THAT MOMS AND KIDS CAN DO TOGETHER WITHOUT WRECKING THE WHOLE HOUSE.

UH....

UMMMM... LET'S SEE... NO, THAT'S MESSY... TOO... UH...

KIRKMAN & SCOTT

OH, NEVER MIND...

I KNEW IT!

BABY BLUES®

BY RICK KIRKMAN / JERRY SCOTT

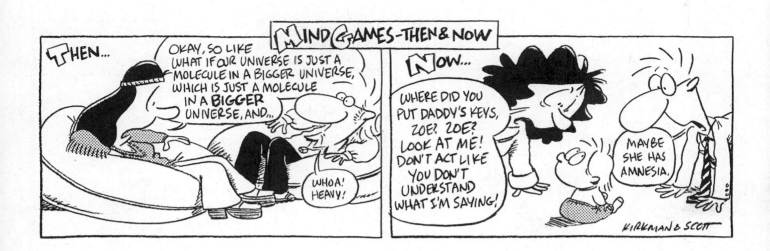

KEEP YOUR MONDAY NIGHTS OPEN FOR THE REST OF THE MONTH... I SIGNED US UP FOR A PARENTING CLASS.

A PARENTING CLASS?

A **PARENTING** CLASS?? I'M THE FATHER OF A TWO-YEAR-OLD, FOR CRYING OUT LOUD! WHAT DO THEY THINK THEY'RE GOING TO TEACH ME?

SENDING ME TO A PARENTING CLASS IS LIKE OFFERING A BATHING CAP TO A GUY GOING OVER A WATERFALL!

WHACK! WHACK! WHACK!

KIRKMAN & SCOTT

LOOK, I'M NOT TRYING TO BE DIFFICULT. I JUST DON'T FEEL LIKE GOING TO A PARENTING CLASS!

GIVE ME ONE GOOD REASON WHY WE SHOULDN'T GO!

GIVE ME ONE GOOD REASON WHY WE **SHOULD!**

FOR THE HEALTH AND WELL-BEING OF OUR CHILDREN!

NO, I MEANT A PETTY, SELFISH REASON LIKE MINE.

KIRKMAN & SCOTT

NO! NO! NOT THIS! **NOT** AGAIN! **NOT** **ME!**

#@!%*! CARDS

CAREFUL WITH YOUR LANGUAGE... SANTA'S WATCHING.

KIRKMAN & SCOTT

BABY BLUES

BY RICK KIRKMAN / JERRY SCOTT

BABY BLUES

BY RICK KIRKMAN / JERRY SCOTT

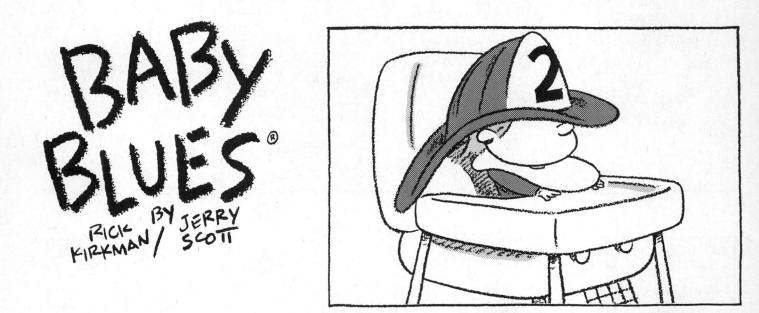

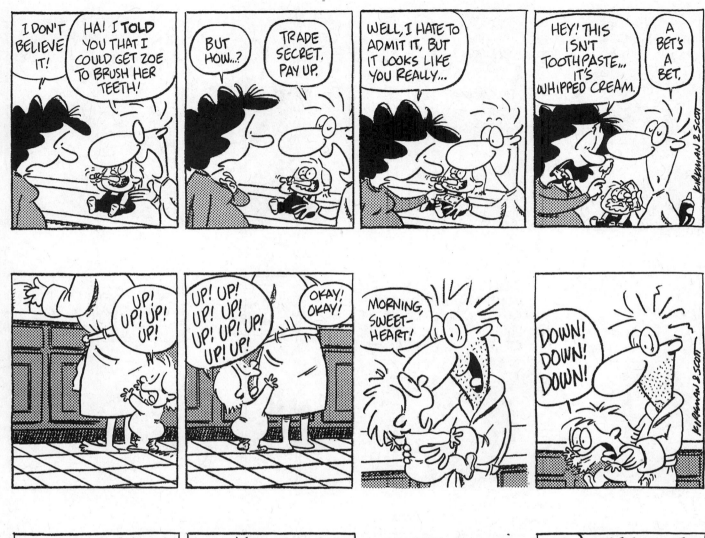

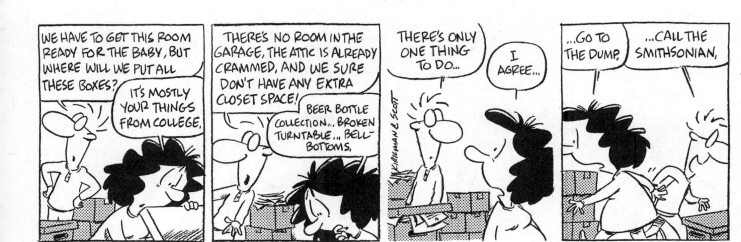

BABY BLUES®

RICK KIRKMAN / JERRY SCOTT BY

75

Panel 1: MOMMY IS REALLY TIRED, ZOE.

Panel 2: WOULD YOU LIKE TO PLAY QUIETLY IN YOUR CRIB, OR TAKE A NAP WITH MOMMY?

Panel 3: HMMM? WHAT WILL IT BE? CRIB, OR NAP WITH ME?
NAP WIF YOU!

Panel 4: MAYBE I SHOULD HAVE PUSHED THE CRIB OPTION A LITTLE HARDER...
Z

KIRKMAN & SCOTT

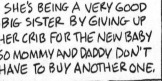

Panel 5: MAY I HELP YOU?
YES. WE'RE LOOKING FOR A BED FOR OUR DAUGHTER.
BEDS! BEDS! BEDS!

Panel 6: SHE'S BEING A VERY GOOD BIG SISTER BY GIVING UP HER CRIB FOR THE NEW BABY SO MOMMY AND DADDY DON'T HAVE TO BUY ANOTHER ONE.

KIRKMAN & SCOTT

Panel 7: I SEE...

Panel 8: ...SO YOU'LL WANT TO TAKE A LOOK AT OUR **BRIBERY SELECTION**...
EXACTLY.

Panel 9: WE HAVE THE **INDY 500** RACE CAR BED COLLECTION, THE **ALICE IN WONDERLAND** CANOPY BED COLLECTION, THE **DR. DOOLITTLE** ANIMAL BED COLLECTION...

Panel 10: WERE YOU LOOKING FOR ANYTHING IN PARTICULAR?
WELL, SORT OF...

Panel 11: HOW ABOUT SOMETHING FROM THE **ONE-INCOME-GROWING FAMILY COLLECTION**?
BACK ROOM... FOLLOW ME.
ZIP!
KIDS BEDS

KIRKMAN & SCOTT

76

BABY BLUES

RICK KIRKMAN / JERRY SCOTT
BY

LOOK AT THIS ROOM! —

THE WHISTLING MONKEY COWBOY BAND COLORING BOOK, WHISTLING MONKEY COWBOY BAND ACTION FIGURES, THEIR TOUR BUS, THEIR STICKER BOOK...

THEIR STUFF IS EVERYWHERE! IT'S ON EVERYTHING! I FEEL LIKE I'M LIVING IN SOME KIND OF THEME PARK!

HA! "WHISTLING MONKEY COWBOY BAND LAND" — THAT'S WHAT THE WORLD NEEDS!

OPENS THIS JUNE. WE HAVE RESERVATIONS.

KIRKMAN & SCOTT

PIKME UP, DA-DA.

JUST A SECOND, ZOE.

I REMEMBER THE DAYS BEFORE SHE COULD TALK, WHEN ALL YOU COULD GET OUT OF HER WAS AN OCCASIONAL "BA" OR MAYBE A GIGGLE.

SO DO I.

PIKME UP! PIKME UP! PIKME UP! PIKME UP! PIKME UP! PIKME UP! PIKME UP! PIKME UP!

KIRKMAN & SCOTT

I MISS THOSE DAYS.

SO DO I.

THE BOOK SAYS WE SHOULD BE PREPARING ZOE FOR THE ARRIVAL OF THE NEW BABY.

HOW?

WELL, THE FIRST THING TO DO IS TO SPEND AS MUCH TIME WITH YOUR CHILD AS POSSIBLE.

CHECK... WHAT ELSE?

KIRKMAN & SCOTT

Panel 1:
WHAT ARE YOU DOING?

PAINTING THE NEW BABY'S CRIB TO MATCH THE WALLS IN HER ROOM.

Panel 2:
WHY DIDN'T YOU TELL ME YOU WERE GOING TO PAINT THE CRIB?

I WANTED IT TO BE A SURPRISE!

Panel 3:
AND IT HASN'T BEEN EASY, EITHER. THE PAINT KEEPS RUNNING, I'VE GOT DRIPS ALL OVER THE PLACE, AND THE BRISTLES KEEP COMING OUT OF THE BRUSH!

KIRKMAN & SCOTT

Panel 4:
I HOPE SHE LIKES IT

I HOPE SHE HAS A SENSE OF HUMOR.

...AND THEN, ONE OF THESE DAYS VERY SOON, THE BABY WILL COME OUT OF MOMMY'S TUMMY AND YOU'LL HAVE A BRAND-NEW BABY SISTER!

KIRKMAN & SCOTT

DO IT NOW.

HEY, THIS IS CHILDBIRTH, NOT A CARD TRICK.

Panel 1:
TODAY I'M GOING TO GET UP, CLEAN THE HOUSE, GO GROCERY SHOPPING, WALK TO THE PARK WITH ZOE, AND COOK A NICE DINNER.

Panel 2:
ERF! UMPH! ARRGH! OOOF!

KIRKMAN & SCOTT

Panel 3:
TODAY, I'M GOING TO GET UP.

BABY BLUES

BY RICK KIRKMAN / JERRY SCOTT

LOOK, ZOE! AUNT RHONDA IS HERE!

ANT WONDA!

ANT WONDA!
ANT WONDA!
ANT WONDA!
ANT WONDA!
≷DING! DONG!€

ANT WONDA! ANT WONDA!
ANT WONDA!
ANT WONDA!

HI, ZOE!

WELCOME TO THE HOUSE OF THE TERRIBLE TWOS.

GO AWAY.

GEE, WANDA... HERE YOU ARE WITH A BEAUTIFUL TWO-YEAR-OLD DAUGHTER AND ANOTHER BABY ON THE WAY.

YOU HAVE A NICE HUSBAND, A HOUSE, REAL FURNITURE...

DID YOU EVER THINK YOUR LIFE WOULD BE SO... SO... SO...

...COMPLETE? FULFILLING? WELL-ROUNDED?

BORING,

BORING?? MY OWN SISTER THINKS I'M **BORING**??

NOT YOU, PERSONALLY... JUST YOUR LIFE.

LOOK— WE MAY STAY HOME A LOT, AND WE MAY BE OBSESSED WITH PARENTHOOD, AND WE MAY GO TO BED EARLY ON THE WEEKENDS, BUT WE ARE **NOT BORING!**

YAHTZEE, ANYONE?

BRAIN DEAD MAYBE, BUT NOT BORING,

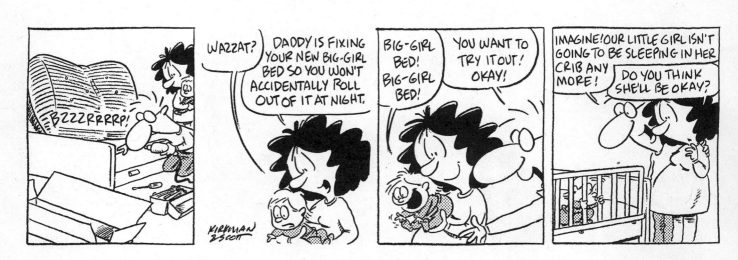

88

BABY BLUES

by RICK KIRKMAN / JERRY SCOTT

HMMM... NOBODY HOME.

WANDA AND ZOE MUST BE AT THE STORE OR SOMETHING.

I GUESS I CAN RELAX FOR A CHANGE!

PHZZT!

WOW! THIS IS WHAT IT USED TO BE LIKE WHEN I CAME HOME FROM WORK BEFORE WE HAD ZOE.

NO NOISE... NO CONFUSION... NO STICKY LITTLE HANDS ALL OVER MY CLOTHES...NOTHING TO DO BUT JUST SIT AND ENJOY THE SOLITUDE.

HOW DID I EVER STAND IT???

91

BABY BLUES®

BY RICK KIRKMAN / JERRY SCOTT

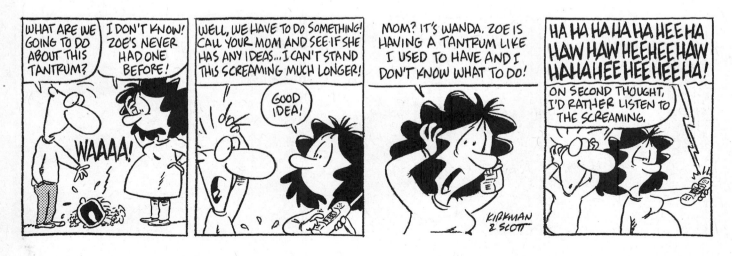

94

Baby Blues®

BY RICK KIRKMAN / JERRY SCOTT

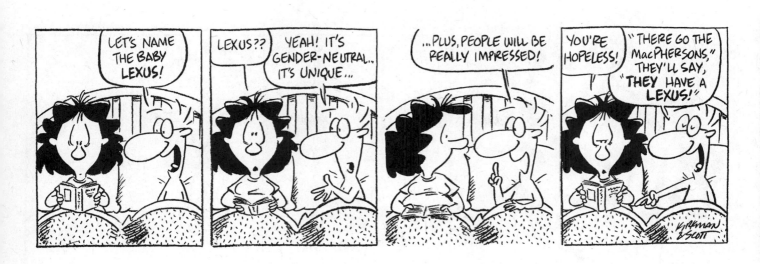

BABY BLUES®

RICK KIRKMAN / BY JERRY SCOTT

HEY! IT'S THE MacPHERSONS!

SO, HOW HAVE YOU BEEN?

FINE, HOW ABOUT YOU?

GOOD! YOU BOTH LOOK GREAT!

YEAH... REALLY GREAT!

SO DO YOU.

SO...WHAT'S NEW?

SAME OL', SAME OL'.

YEAH... US, TOO.

WELL, WE HAVE TO GET GOING... LET'S GET TOGETHER SOON.

WAAAAAAAAAAAAAA

SOUNDS GOOD. WE'LL CALL YOU.

BYE, GUYS!

REMEMBER WHEN WE HAD TIME TO LOOK AT PEOPLE WHEN WE TALKED TO THEM?

WHAT PEOPLE?

SNIF

KIRKMAN & SCOTT

105

106

MAYBE WE SHOULD NAME THE BABY AFTER SOMEONE FAMOUS!

WHEN I WAS A KID, I HAD A CRUSH ON URSULA ANDRESS, THE ACTRESS.

URSULA??

COME TO THINK OF IT, I ALSO HAD CRUSHES ON CLAUDIA CARDINALE, RAQUEL WELCH, VANESSA REDGRAVE AND ANNETTE FUNICELLO...

KIRKMAN & SCOTT

HOW ABOUT URSULA-CLAUDIA-RAQUEL-VANESSA-ANNETTE MacPHERSON?

HOW ABOUT NONE-OF-THE ABOVE?

HEY! WHAT ABOUT "MANDY" FOR THE NEW BABY'S NAME?

MANDY, HUH? HMMM...

I KNEW A MANDY IN HIGH SCHOOL. WHAT A BABE!

WE WENT OUT A FEW TIMES, BOY! TALK ABOUT A... UH, WELL, NEVER MIND.

KIRKMAN & SCOTT

MANDY'S FINE.

FORGET "MANDY"...

SCRATCH!

NO LABOR PAINS AT ALL TODAY?

NONE.

NOT EVEN A TWINGE! NOTHING! ZERO! ZILCH! NADA!

TODAY IS MY DUE DATE! I'M READY, YOU'RE READY, THE DOCTOR AND THE HOSPITAL ARE READY... EVERYONE IS WAITING!

SHE'S NOT EVEN BORN YET, AND THIS KID IS ALREADY MAKING US LATE!

KIRKMAN & SCOTT

Baby Blues®

BY RICK KIRKMAN / JERRY SCOTT

GURK!

WANDA— I THINK YOU JUST HAD A CONTRACTION!

GEE, THANKS... IF YOU HADN'T NOTICED— I MIGHT HAVE MISSED IT!

LABOR ALWAYS MAKES YOU SARCASTIC, YOU KNOW THAT?

KIRKMAN & SCOTT

DON'T WORRY ABOUT A THING, YOU GUYS. ZOE WILL BE JUST FINE HERE WITH ME.

AND YOU HANG IN THERE, SIS. I KNOW EXACTLY WHAT YOU'RE GOING THROUGH.

I WAS THERE WHEN MUFFIN HAD HER PUPPIES, TOO, REMEMBER?

KIRKMAN & SCOTT

YOU'RE RIGHT... SHE DOES GET SARCASTIC WHEN SHE'S IN LABOR!

AND LOUD.

OKAY, HONEY. I'LL GET THE PAPERWORK FILLED OUT AND THEN MEET YOU IN THE ROOM.

OKAY.

ADMITTING

I LOVE YOU.

I LOVE YOU.

ADMITTING

SNIFF!

KIRKMAN & SCOTT

FIRST BABY?

NO, SECOND BABY... SAME INSURANCE.

Baby Blues®

RICK KIRKMAN / JERRY SCOTT BY

BABY BLUES®

BY RICK KIRKMAN / JERRY SCOTT

QUIET HOSPITAL ZONE

HERE COMES THE SON
SUNG TO THE TUNE OF THE BEATLES' "HERE COMES THE SUN"

HERE COMES A SON (doo 'n doo-doo)
HERE COMES A SON,
AND I SAY, "IT'S A FRIGHT!"

LITTLE DARLIN', IT WAS A
SHOCK TO SEE YOUR GENDER!
LITTLE DARLIN', WE THOUGHT
A GIRL WAS TO APPEAR!

HERE COMES A SON (doo 'n doo-doo)
WE'RE BOTH SO STUNNED,
AND I SAY, "YOU'RE A SIGHT!"

KIRKMAN & SCOTT

LITTLE DARLIN', THE BLOOD'S
RETURNING TO OUR FACES.
LITTLE DARLIN', WE SEE THE YEARS
THAT YOU'LL BE HERE.

HE IS OUR SON.
LOOK WHAT WE'VE DONE,
AND I SAY, "HE'S JUST RIGHT."

SON, SON, SON, HERE WE COME!
SON, SON, SON - OF-A-GUN!
SON, SON, SON, HERE WE COME!
SON, SON, SON-OF-A-GUN!
SON, SON, SON, HERE WE COME!

LITTLE DARLIN', YOUR VERY
FIRST SUNRISE IS DAWNING.
LITTLE DARLIN', IT'S JUST AN
HOUR SINCE YOU GOT HERE.

HERE COMES THE SUN (doo 'n doo-doo)
WE HAVE A SON,
AND I SAY, "IT'S SO RIGHT!"

HERE COMES THE SUN (doo 'n doo-doo)
WE HAVE A SON.
IT'S SO RIGHT!
IT'S SO RIGHT!

(WITH APOLOGIES TO
GEORGE HARRISON)

117

BABY BLUES

RICK KIRKMAN BY JERRY SCOTT

HOW CAN WE BE OUT OF DIAPERS ALREADY?

THEY GO THROUGH 'EM FAST AT THIS AGE, REMEMBER?

WE SHOULD GO TO DISCOUNT JUNGLE, BUT DO YOU THINK IT WOULD BE OKAY TO BRING THE BABY WITH US?

SURE... WHY NOT?

YOU KNOW, WITH ALL THE PEOPLE THERE I WORRY ABOUT THE GERMS.

OH, COME ON... IT'LL BE FINE.

HE CAN'T HAVE **THAT** MANY GERMS.

I MEANT EVERYBODY ELSE'S GERMS!

KIRKMAN & SCOTT

OKAY, THEY HAVE CUDDLES, POOCHIES, BUNCHIES, DIAPIES, GUNKIES AND THE STORE BRAND... WHICH ONES DO YOU LIKE?

DISPOSABLE DIAPERS

DISCOUNT JUNGLE

I DON'T KNOW... THEY ALL LOOK ABOUT THE SAME. WHAT'S THE DIFFERENCE?

KIRKMAN 2 SCOTT

DISCOUNT JUNGLE DIAPERS

THIS END UP

WITH THE STORE BRAND YOU GET MORE.

THAT'S A LOT OF DIAPERS.

≥UNNH! AGH!≥ IT SURE IS!

DISCOUNT JUNGLE DIAPERS

CONTENTS ONE BALE

KIRKMAN 2 SCOTT

DO YOU THINK WE NEED THAT MANY?

WE WILL EVENTUALLY.

DISCOUNT JUNGLE DIAPERS

THIS END UP

THAT'S THE BEAUTY OF ≥OOF!≥ BUYING IN BULK... WITH THIS NUMBER OF DIAPERS, THE UNIT COST IS ≥ERF!≥ ABOUT HALF WHAT THE GROCERY STORES CHARGE.

DISCOUNT JUNGLE DIAPERS

CONTENTS: ONE BALE

THIS END

OF COURSE, WHEN YOU FIGURE IN THE COST OF THE HERNIA OPERATION, IT PROBABLY COMES OUT EVEN.

YOU MAY BE RIGHT.

THIS END UP

126

The End